MACHINES AT WORK

On the Building Site

IAN GRAHAM

QED Publishing

First published in the UK in 2006 by
QED Publishing
A Quarto Group company
226 City Road
London EC1V 2TT
www.qed-publishing.co.uk

A Catalogue record for this book is available from the British Library.

ISBN 978 1 84538 471 5

Printed and bound in China

Picture credits

Key: t = top, b = bottom, c = centre, l = left, r = right, FC = front cover

Alamy/Ace Stock 4-5, /Eric Nathan 10CR, /Maximillian Weinzierl 10-11; Ross W Boulanger/Geotechnical Engineering 23T, /
32-33 David J. Green; Construction Photography/Adrian Greeman 14-15; Corbis 32BL, /Craig Aurness 14BL, /
Gehl Company 23CR, /David Sailors 15BL; Freefoto/Ian Britton 5C, 25CR, 30-31; Getty Images/Paul Chesley 28-29, /
Reza Estakhrian 5TR, /Bruce Forster 11CL, /Lester Lefkowitz 9BL, /Malcolm Piers 24-25, /Terje Rakke 6-7; Hochtief
Aktiengesellschaft 17B; JCB 7BR, 12-13; Komatsu Ltd 3, 13BC; Liebherr International 8-9, 22, 28BR; P & H Mining
Equipment 27TL, / Bob Peters 20TR; SOA Photolibrary/Cornelius Meffert/Stem 26-27; Volvo FC, 7TR, 13TL, 29TR, 31TL

Words in **bold** can be found in the glossary on page 34.

CONTENTS

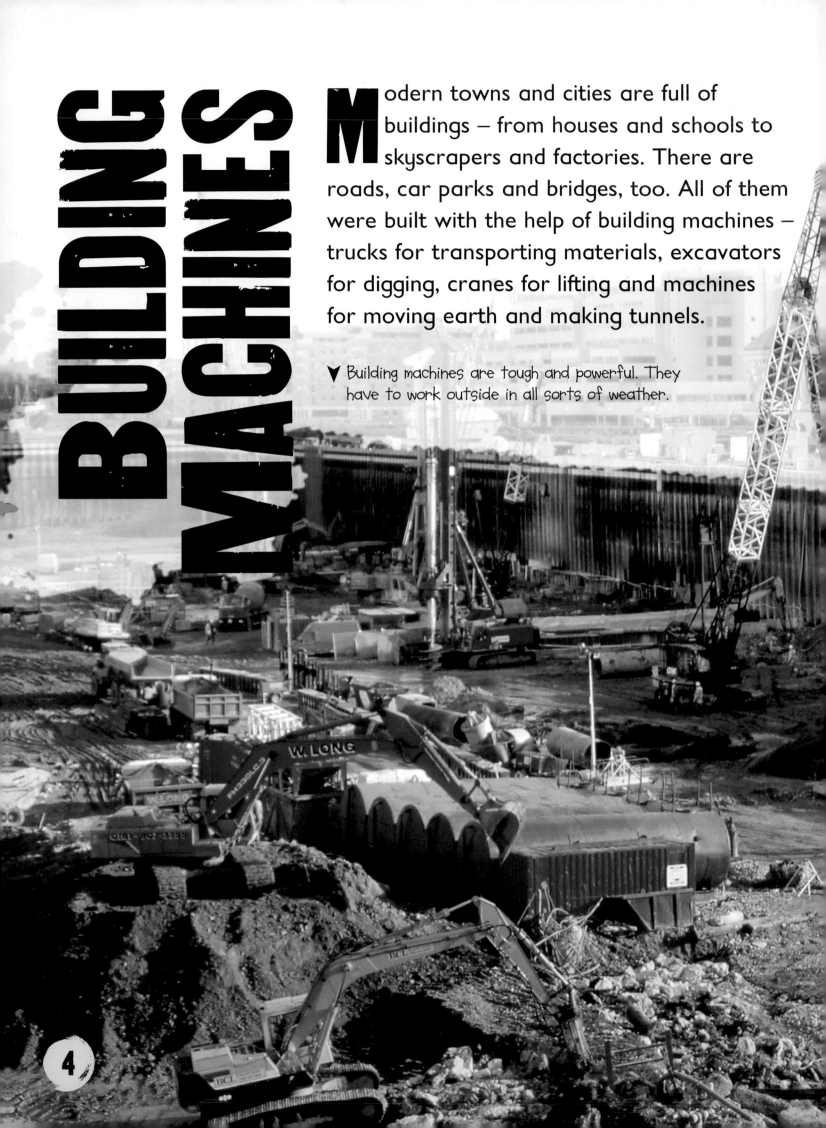

BUILDING MACHINES

Modern towns and cities are full of buildings – from houses and schools to skyscrapers and factories. There are roads, car parks and bridges, too. All of them were built with the help of building machines – trucks for transporting materials, excavators for digging, cranes for lifting and machines for moving earth and making tunnels.

▼ Building machines are tough and powerful. They have to work outside in all sorts of weather.

Machine power

Lots of earth must be moved to build modern roads, bridges and buildings. In the past, large numbers of people did this groundwork and it took a long time. Today, the power of machines makes it possible to do this type of work in a fraction of the time.

Many modern building projects ➤ would not be possible without building machines.

THROUGH THE AIR

A big building site is a jumble of machines, materials and workers. Everywhere are piles of earth, sand and gravel. The quickest way to move heavy materials around the site is to lift them up and carry them through the air. Big building sites have many cranes for this work.

▲ Tall cranes tower high above a building site.

DIGGERS

Diggers, or **excavators**, of all sizes are widely used on building sites. They dig holes for the **foundations** of buildings and bridges, as well as trenches for water pipes, **power cables** and drains. A big **bucket** on the end of a **mechanical arm** digs up the dirt. The arm has joints like your arm, but it is much bigger and stronger.

The bucket on the front of this ➤ huge digger is designed to scoop up large amounts of earth and rock.

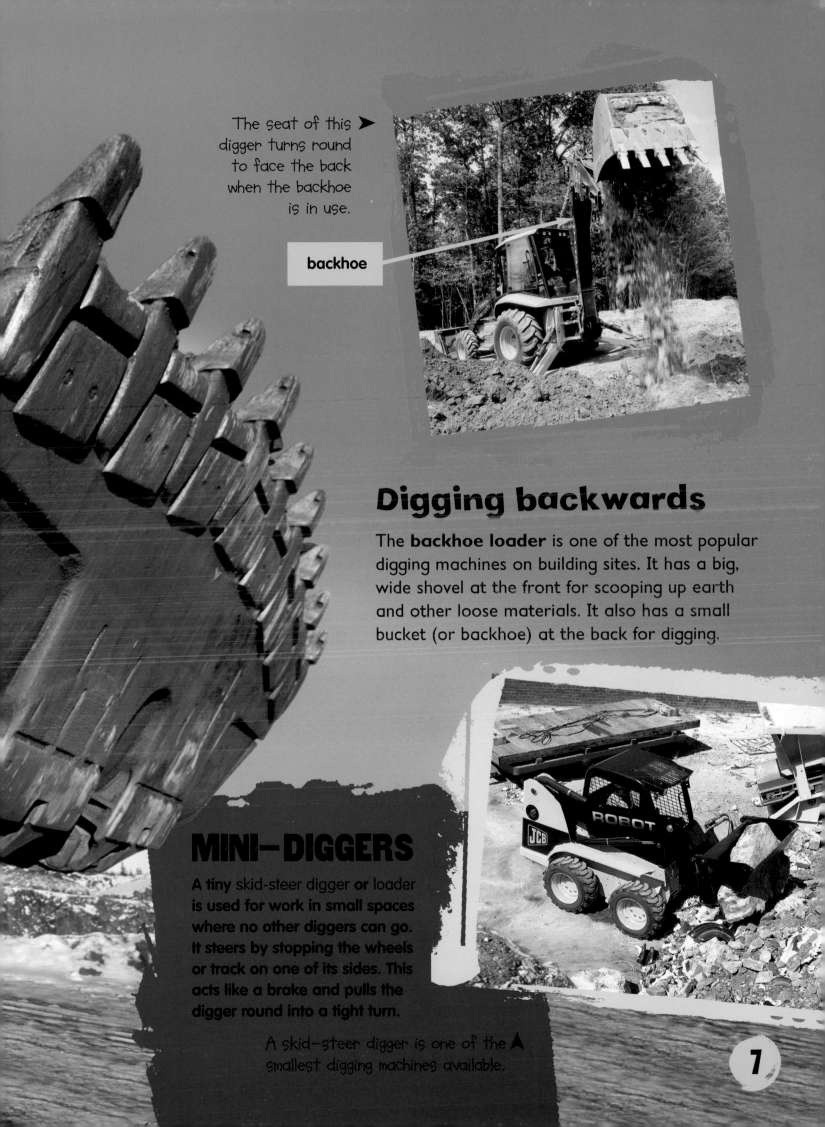

The seat of this ➤ digger turns round to face the back when the backhoe is in use.

backhoe

Digging backwards

The **backhoe loader** is one of the most popular digging machines on building sites. It has a big, wide shovel at the front for scooping up earth and other loose materials. It also has a small bucket (or backhoe) at the back for digging.

MINI-DIGGERS

A tiny skid-steer digger or loader is used for work in small spaces where no other diggers can go. It steers by stopping the wheels or track on one of its sides. This acts like a brake and pulls the digger round into a tight turn.

A skid-steer digger is one of the ▲ smallest digging machines available.

CONCRETE MIXERS

Huge amounts of concrete are used on a building site. Concrete is a mixture of sand, gravel, cement and water. It can be poured, moulded and spread and sets rock hard. Concrete is delivered to building sites by **concrete mixer trucks**. These have a large drum on top to hold the concrete. The truck's engine slowly turns the drum, and blades inside churn up the mixture.

PUMPING OUT

If the chute at the back of a concrete mixer truck doesn't stretch to where it is needed on a building site, a machine called a concrete pump is used. The mixer truck pours its concrete into a tank at the back of the concrete pump. The pump then forces the concrete out through a long pipe.

◄ A concrete pump carries concrete to exactly where it is needed.

▼ The drum of a concrete mixer truck must keep turning or the concrete will set hard inside it.

▲ Concrete flows out of the mixer and down a chute onto the ground.

Unloading

To unload concrete, the driver reverses the direction of the drum. The curved blades that mixed the concrete then turn in the opposite direction. This pushes the mixture out of the drum and down a chute at the back of the mixer.

DEMOLITION

Old buildings often have to be **demolished** before work on new buildings can begin. Excavators can be fitted with different tools that can break up a building piece by piece.

The digging bucket ➤ of this excavator can also be used to pull down walls.

Breakers

An excavator's digging bucket can be removed and replaced with useful demolition tools. Apart from a concrete crusher, it can be fitted with a **hammer**, or breaker. Driven by high-pressure air, the hammer can smash up concrete.

▲ A concrete crusher, or **pulverizer**, can eat through walls like a metal dinosaur!

A building that took months to build can be brought down in seconds at the press of a button.

3, 2, 1 ...BANG!

Large buildings are demolished by blowing them up. Explosives are placed in the building to blow out the walls and pillars that hold it up. Then the weight of the building brings down the rest of the structure. The explosives are not all set off at once. They are set off in a carefully planned order so that the building falls down in exactly the right direction and does not damage any other nearby buildings.

EARTH MOVERS

A lot of groundwork has to be done before building begins on a site. The ground may need to be levelled and piles of earth may need to be moved to build roads and bridges. Certain machines are designed to do this hard work. **Bulldozers** push big piles of earth around, **scrapers** shave bumps off rough ground and **compactors** press down loose earth with their heavy wheels.

Dump trucks ➤
move earth around
building sites.

FLATTENING EARTH

Bulldozers and scrapers are followed by machines called graders. These are strange-looking vehicles. A grader is like a tractor with a sharp blade underneath. As the grader moves along, the blade scrapes up any bumps of earth and stones that stick up.

▲ Graders shave the last bumps off the ground and make a flat, smooth surface that can be built on.

▼ A bulldozer scrapes up earth and pushes it to where it is needed.

FACT!

The biggest bulldozer in the world is the Komatsu D575. Its blade is more than 7m wide (that's the length of two cars) and nearly 3m high. Bulldozers this big are called super-dozers.

TUNNELLING MACHINES

In the past, all tunnels were dug by men using picks and shovels. Explosives were used to blast out solid rock. Today, only the smallest tunnels are still dug by hand. The larger tunnels needed for underground railways are dug by giant tunnelling machines. These machines have a cutting head at the front covered with sharp metal wheels or teeth.

A modern tunnelling ➤ machine, being prepared for action, towers over the workers.

Tiny tunnels

Small tunnels are too narrow for a digging machine to fit inside. These tunnels are dug with the help of air-powered hand-drills, also called **pneumatic drills**. High-pressure air punches the sharp end of the drill into the rock many times a second, chipping the rock away.

▲ Rock drills like this are powered by air instead of electricity.

FINISHING OFF

Even small tunnels have to be given a hard lining to stop loose rock falling into the tunnel. First, wire mesh is fixed in place all round the tunnel. Concrete is then sprayed onto it. Finally, long bolts are screwed through the lining into the surrounding rock to hold it in place.

◄ Wire mesh gives the tunnel lining extra strength.

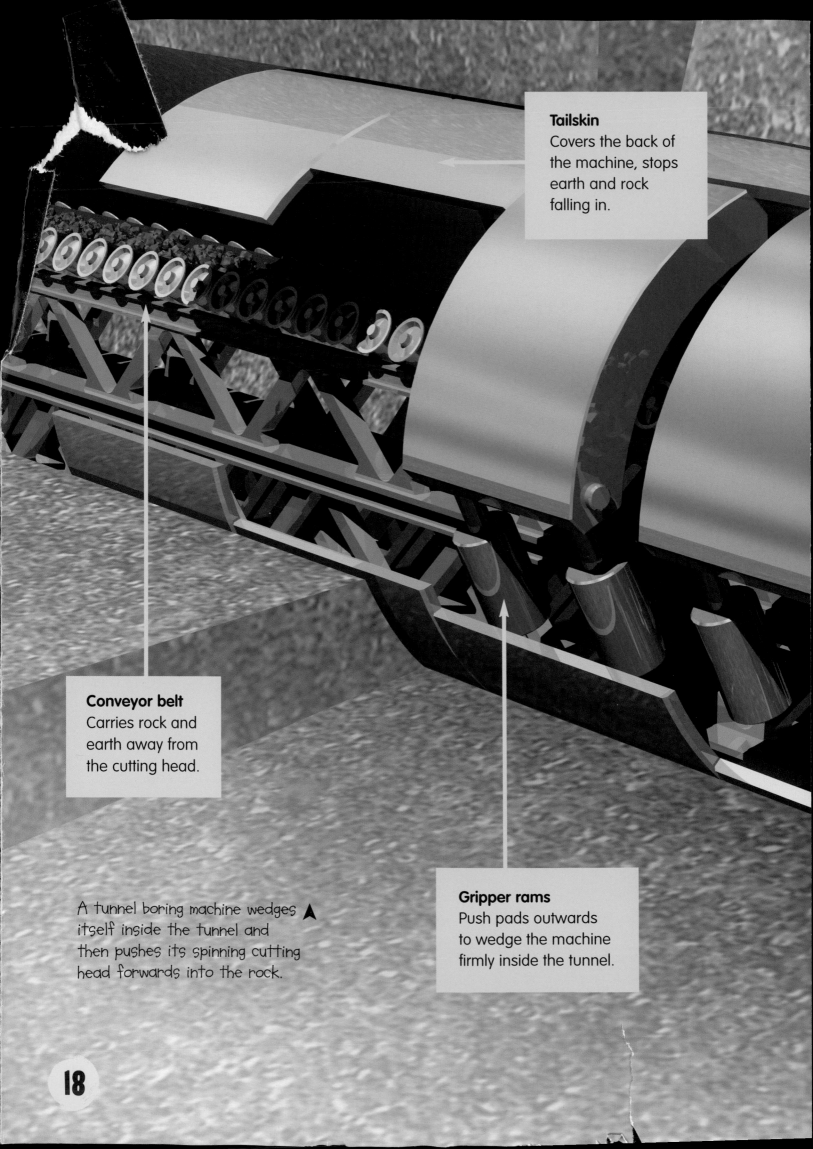

Tailskin
Covers the back of the machine, stops earth and rock falling in.

Conveyor belt
Carries rock and earth away from the cutting head.

A tunnel boring machine wedges itself inside the tunnel and then pushes its spinning cutting head forwards into the rock.

Gripper rams
Push pads outwards to wedge the machine firmly inside the tunnel.

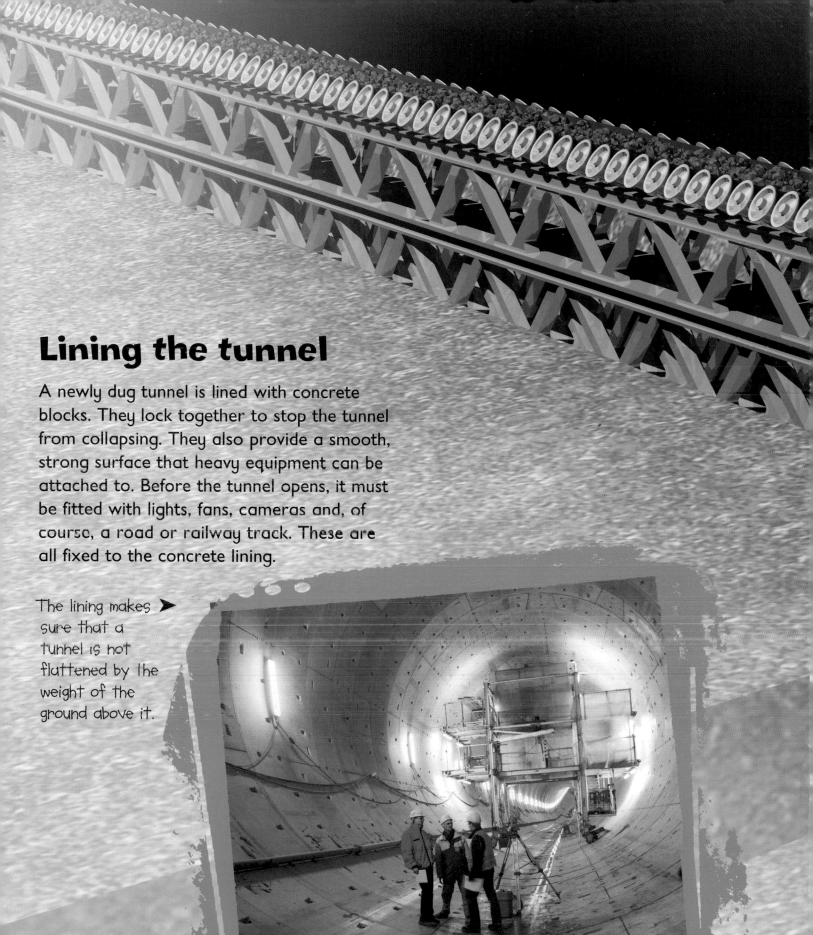

Lining the tunnel

A newly dug tunnel is lined with concrete blocks. They lock together to stop the tunnel from collapsing. They also provide a smooth, strong surface that heavy equipment can be attached to. Before the tunnel opens, it must be fitted with lights, fans, cameras and, of course, a road or railway track. These are all fixed to the concrete lining.

The lining makes ➤ sure that a tunnel is not flattened by the weight of the ground above it.

MECHANICAL MOLES

The longest tunnels are dug by special **tunnel boring machines**, or TBMs. A TBM moves through the ground like a giant mechanical mole, carving out the tunnel as it goes. The machine locks itself in one place inside the tunnel and pushes a cutting head forwards to cut through the rock.

The spinning cutting head of the TBM bites into the rock to carve out the tunnel. The cutting head is covered in dozens of sharp wheels or teeth-like cutters called picks. The picks bite into the rock and carve out the tunnel.

Power train

A vehicle called a **service train** travels behind a tunnel boring machine inside the tunnel. An on-board generator makes electricity, which powers the tunnelling machine. It also removes earth and rock dug out by the TBM and helps to line the tunnel wall.

▲ Rock cut away by the TBM falls onto a moving conveyor belt inside the service train. It drops into railway wagons at the end of the train and the wagons take it away.

FACT!

The Channel Tunnel rail link between England and France was built using 11 TBMs. The biggest of them weighed more than 1500 tonnes and, together with its service train, measured over 250m long — that's the length of 25 double-decker buses!

PILES OF WORK

It is very important that a building stands on firm ground, otherwise it might lean over or even fall down! The famous Leaning Tower of Pisa in Italy leans because its weight squashes the ground more on one side than the other.

Tall buildings stand up straight today because they are built on top of long 'pegs' called **piles** that are driven deep underground.

Driving piles into ➤ the ground is one of the first jobs to be done on a building site.

pile

From the ground up

When the foundations of a big building are finished, rows of steel bars stick out from the tops of the piles. A grid of steel bars is then built over the piles. Then concrete is poured over it all to lock the base of the building to the piles.

◀ The steel bars that run through concrete are called rebars. This means 'reinforcing bars', because the bars reinforce, or strengthen, the concrete.

BORING WORK

Another way to make piles is to bore holes into the ground and then fill them with steel and concrete. A machine called an auger bores holes by screwing itself into the ground. When it is pulled out, the earth comes out with it. Then the hole is filled in again with concrete and steel.

▲ An auger looks like a giant screw. A motor turns it and screws it into the ground.

CRANES

Heavy materials have to be moved around on building sites. **Tower cranes** are the machines for this job. These cranes have a metal tower with a boom, or arm, balanced on top. The load is lifted by a hook at one end of the boom. The weight of the load is balanced by another heavy weight on the opposite side of the tower.

Travelling cranes

A **mobile crane** is a crane on a truck. Before it lifts anything, legs called **outriggers** come out from its sides and push down onto the ground. These keep the crane level and make it wider so that the load it lifts will not pull it over.

boom

hook

operator's cab

The Millennium Bridge in Gateshead weighs 850 tonnes. It was lifted into position by Europe's largest floating crane, Asian Hercules II.

Tower cranes ➤ do all the heavy lifting work on building sites.

UNDERWATER LIFTING

If a sunken boat needs to be lifted or a bridge has to be raised into position over a river, a floating crane may be used. This sort of crane sits on top of a floating barge.

FACT!
The world's biggest floating crane is Saipem 7000. It can lift an amazing 14 000 tonnes!

Bachy (UK) Ltd.

LAND GIANTS

Many materials and products used in the building industry are made from raw materials that are found underground. These are dug out of the ground by giant digging machines. One of the biggest of these is the **bucket wheel excavator**.

FACT!

The world's biggest bucket wheel excavator is also the biggest vehicle of any kind. The MAN Takraf RB293 weighs 14 000 tonnes and each of its buckets is as big as a car!

WALKING DIGGERS

Dragline excavators have a huge bucket that dangles from a cable at the end of a long boom. The bucket is used to dig up earth. It is lowered onto the ground and dragged towards the excavator, scraping up earth as it goes. The biggest dragline excavators move by walking on giant metal feet.

▲ This dragline bucket holds enough earth to fill more than 200 bath tubs.

▲ Amazingly, the biggest bucket wheel excavators weigh as much as 10 000 cars! This machine digs by using a special wheel with buckets. As the wheel turns, the buckets dig into the ground and scoop up earth.

SUPER HAULERS

Huge amounts of soil and rock are hauled out of mines and made into cement and other materials used for building. The hauling work is done by **mine trucks**. These **off-road trucks** never travel on ordinary roads, which means they can be huge. The biggest are called **ultra trucks**.

▲ Ultra trucks are so tall that the driver is less than half the height of one tyre!

A GIANT PROBLEM

Ultra trucks are enormous. The cab is so far off the ground that the driver has to climb a ladder to get up to it! These trucks are so huge that the drivers can't see behind them. Some trucks have video cameras, with screens in the cab so the driver can see what is behind and around him.

Unloading

Trucks empty out their load by tipping up the back of the truck so the contents slide onto the ground. The biggest dump trucks can empty out more than 360 tonnes of earth in just 30 seconds.

It takes enormous power ➤ to lift the back of a full truck and empty it.

▼ The biggest trucks on Earth are used in the mining industry. Some are as big as a house.

ROAD TRUCKS

All sorts of building materials are delivered to building sites by trucks. Loose materials such as sand, gravel and soil are delivered by dump trucks. These are smaller than the giant dump trucks used in mining, because they have to travel on ordinary roads. Some trucks are **rigid**. Others bend behind the driver's cab. The bendy trucks are known as **articulated trucks**.

A dump truck ➤ transports loose materials such as soil in a big box called a hopper.

Wooden platforms

Heavy items transported by truck are often carried on wooden platforms called pallets. The pallets have a space underneath so they can be lifted easily by a forklift truck.

▲ Forklift trucks are often used to unload goods from delivery trucks.

ROAD-BUILDING MACHINES

The machines that build roads are called **pavement layers**, or pavers. Small stones and a thick, black, oily substance called **asphalt**, or **bitumen**, are loaded into a pavement layer. The machine mixes the stones and hot asphalt together. As it moves along slowly, the paver spreads the mixture on the ground to make a new road.

A pavement-laying ▲ machine spreads steaming hot asphalt onto the ground.

A machine called a **road roller** follows the ▶ pavement layer. As it drives up and down the road, its heavy rollers flatten and harden the newly laid road surface.

GLOSSARY

articulated truck a truck that can bend in the middle

asphalt a black substance that is used to make road surfaces

auger a screw-shaped tool that can drill holes into the ground

backhoe loader a vehicle with a scooping bucket at the front and a digging bucket at the back

bitumen like asphalt, a black substance that is used to make road surfaces

boom the long arm on a crane

bucket the part of a digging machine that scoops up earth

bucket wheel excavator a large digging machine with a huge wheel at the front to which lots of buckets are attached. As the wheel turns, the buckets dig up dirt

bulldozer a powerful machine with a large blade at the front which can push huge amounts of earth

compactor a heavy vehicle driven across soft earth to squash it down and make it harder

compressor an engine-driven pump that pushes air through a pipe into a tool such as a road drill

concrete mixer truck a truck that has a large, round container on its back in which cement is mixed

conveyor belt a moving belt that is used to move goods or materials from place to place

cutting head a part of a machine with sharp wheels or teeth for slicing through the ground

demolish pull down or destroy

dump truck a truck with a large container called a hopper on the back, that is emptied by tipping it up

excavator a digging machine

foundations the bottom layer of a building. Foundations make a level, strong surface on which the rest of a building can be built

grader a vehicle with a sharp blade underneath. The blade smoothes out bumps on the ground as the grader drives along

hammer an air-driven tool that fits on the end of an excavator's arm instead of a digging bucket. It is used to break up concrete

loader a vehicle with a bucket that is used to scoop soil or other loose materials off the ground. The material is then loaded into a truck

mechanical arm a metal arm that is worked by a machine

mine trucks large trucks that dig up and carry materials from mines

mobile crane a crane with wheels that can travel by road

off-road truck a truck that works on rough ground. Some off-road trucks never travel on roads

outriggers strong metal legs that reach out from the side of a machine or a vehicle to give it a wider base and so make it steadier

pavement layer a machine that lays a new road surface

piles long metal or concrete pillars that are sunk into the ground to provide supports on which a building can be constructed

pneumatic drill a powerful drill operated by compressed air

power cables lengths of wire that carry electricity to a building

pulverizer a machine that crushes something completely

rigid something that does not bend

road header a machine that makes tunnels by grinding through rock

road roller a machine that flattens and hardens the surface of a newly laid road

scraper a machine that moves earth by scraping it up into a big box called a hopper

service train the railway train that follows a tunnel boring machine and provides it with power

skid-steer digger a small digging machine that steers by stopping the wheels or track on one side, also called a skid loader

tower crane a crane that sits on top of a tall metal tower

tunnel boring machine (TBM) a machine designed to cut its way through the ground to create a tunnel

ultra truck any of the world's biggest trucks. Ultra trucks are used in the mining industry

FIND OUT MORE

Websites

Find out more about trucks, diggers, bulldozers and other building machines and vehicles:
www.kenkenkikki.jp/zukan/e_index.html

Discover out how a tower crane is built and how it works:
http://science.howstuffworks.com/tower-crane.htm

Learn all about mobile cranes:
http://science.howstuffworks.com/hydraulic-crane.htm

Read about skid-steer diggers:
http://science.howstuffworks.com/skid-steer.htm

Discover the history and facts about demolishing buildings by explosives:
http://www.implosionworld.com

Find out how a building is demolished by explosives:
http://science.howstuffworks.com/building-implosion.htm

INDEX